uin de

st barr

GW00356792

Of L

and Carre Latte

Mark Greene spent a decade working in advertising on both sides of the Atlantic and is prepared to admit it. He has lectured in communications, contemporary culture and creative writing and is now the Director of the London Institute for Contemporary Christianity, a think and response unit on issues facing people today. He has written a book on work called *Thank God it's Monday*, and a collection of poems called *Opening Night*.

Mark enjoys ham acting, occasional humiliations on the dance floor and more frequent ones on the squash court. He has Scottish parents, was brought up Jewish and is married to a Finn called Katriina. And they have three young and exuberant children who seem splendidly secure in their identity.

Of Love, Life
and Caffè Latte

MARK GREENE

AZURE

First published in Great Britain in 2000
Azure
1 Marylebone Road
London NW1 4DU

British Library Cataloguing-in-Publication Data

A catalogue record for this book is available
from the British Library

ISBN 1–902694–10–4

Typeset by Pioneer Associates, Perthshire
Printed in Great Britain by
Caledonian International, Glasgow

Contents

For:

Jaana Katriina Metso Greene
Reine de Mon Coeur

With thanks to my bevy of editors:

Kamal of Ethos who likes risks and developing other people's taste in them.

Gareth erstwhile of Christianity who sees things differently and likes changing other people's lenses.

Alison of Azure who has a cordon bleu's instinct for knowing that a little soupçon here and a little restraint there can make all the difference.

Dan of the London Institute for Contemporary Christianity who knows what he likes and what he doesn't and says so nicely.

1
A Little Gas with a Petrol Pump

Yesterday I talked to a petrol pump

You know how it is – when it comes to relationships you take what you can get. He, I guess it was a 'he' – rather task-focused in his communication, concise, crisp, and in need of a good scrub – but it's tough to tell these days. Anyway, 'he' was polite, recognized me from my card and did everything that I wanted in rather less time than it takes to exchange two 'how are you's' and a smile. He didn't smile but he did give me three bright yellow little blinks. That was nice but I suppose he does that for all the guys.

Last week I talked to a hole in the wall

At least that's what it must have looked like from a distance. Or maybe people just thought I was in

France. Anyway the hole in the wall is much more loquacious. If you press all the right buttons you can spend maybe a whole five minutes chattering away. I like the hole in the wall. 'It' offers lots of options, is very polite, tells me pretty much anything I want to know and makes friendly whirring noises while we're chatting. I think 'it' is a 'she'. She's always rather neat and never smells of Castrol GTX.

A while back I was in a traffic jam

Watford. Saturday afternoon. On my right, Wickes. The radio isn't working. Or rather it probably is but we have some new-fangled aerial with a special release system and I haven't worked out how to release it. I get to thinking. You know how it is, you don't have the dosh for a cassette or a CD, and there's nothing else to do, and you're cut off from 178 radio stations, and you're hanging around in traffic jams, and pretty soon you catch yourself thinking. Anyway, I'm thinking: if I wanted to go into Wickes right now and pick up a tin of clear varnish and they didn't have it, well, what would I have to do? I'd have to get back in the car, crawl round the one-way system for 25 minutes and betake myself to B&Q. And when I get to the checkout, there will be somebody there whom I have never seen before and will probably never see again. Then I'd remember that we needed a carton of milk, two pounds of apples and a tube of sunscreen and I'd have to crawl round the one-way system for 25 minutes and do the Tesco-dodgems. And when I get to the checkout, there will be somebody there whom I have never seen before and will probably never see again.

Pretty soon I'm getting nostalgic. I'm remembering that when 'I were a lad', a ten-year-old lad in leafy, suburban Northwood, I would walk down the road to the shops with the little shopping list my mum had given me and my little brother. I'd stop in at Allen's the fruit shop, and they'd know my name, without looking at my card, and they'd read my list and write the prices by the items, and pop the fruit into the brown paper bags and twirl them round and round so that they ended up with two little pigtails sticking up in the air. And then I'd go to the supermarket which was about the size of your average domestic double garage. And then across to Mr Worbuoy, the butcher, and then up to the bread shop on the bridge. And if my dad wanted a tin of clear varnish I would run over to Carey's and they would have it. They had everything in that Aladdin's cave and they would put it on Mr Greene's account and not even ask me for any ID. It was kind of nice and kind of safe. And I realize that there is no way my son will ever be going down to the shops with a little list and his little brother, buying fruit and meat and varnish from people whose names he knows and who know his. I realize that those shops hardly exist any longer – most of them have turned into hair-dressers or boutiques or restaurants. And anyway even if they did, you just don't let ten year olds out into suburbia on their own with a purse full of money.

I'm in the local park with my two little boys - 5 and 2

A little clutch of ten year olds arrive – three or four boys. They pick up some stones and start to throw them at some girls in the playground 30, 40 yards away. There's another adult standing ten yards away from the boys. One of the boys has a good arm and the stones are getting close.

We're silent

And I get to thinking. Thirty years ago, ten-year-old boys would not be throwing stones at young girls in the presence of two male adults. Thirty years ago one of us would have already told them to stop and clipped them one round the ear hole. And nobody would have sued as a result. Thirty years ago I would have done it and I wouldn't have been afraid that if I said something those ten year olds would turn on me and beat me up and start throwing stones at my kids. But I am afraid. But I think: 'If not me, who?' And anyway, what will my kids conclude if I do nothing?

So, as another volley of stones whizzes through the air, I say something. It feels dangerous. Absurdly, depressingly, it *feels* like heroism. They answer back. (Oh, to be talking to a petrol pump – petrol pumps never answer back.) The boys ask, 'Why not?' In a moment of unpredictable eloquence I say, 'If you live by the stone, you die by the stone.' The word 'die' probably intrigues them. 'What does that mean?' the chief of the Exocets demands. I explain. They're not impressed. They are resentful but they've stopped throwing stones.

The other adult comments, 'When I was a lad I'd never have talked back to an adult like that.'

'No, nor would I.'

But then we cared about one another. We knew the name of the man in the fruit shop. And he knew ours.

2
Sex and the City

Call me a masochist but I've always wanted to be a fly on the wall listening to a group of women talk about life, love and men – without any men around. I'm not sure why I'd want to be there; I'm not sure it would be pleasurable; it might wreak permanent psychological damage. I'm not sure if they'd even be honest with one another – men aren't necessarily more honest when there aren't any women around – but, hey, as one of the things I want to do before I go knock, knock, knockin' on heaven's door, it's right up there with Red Army Cossack dancing, dinner with Germaine Greer and writing a spy novel. I guess with all this hi-tech surveillance equipment around I might have simply bugged a few friends' sitting rooms, even my own, but the money seemed better spent on the TV licence. Anyway, *Sex and the City* was supposed to deliver this delectable pleasure to me without requiring me to develop wings, compound eyes, four legs or call in 'Q'. And it did. But could I believe it?

Certainly, *Sex and the City* was much heralded and much dreaded but when it arrived it hit Channel 4's increasingly prurient menu with all the impact of a marshmallow on Lennox Lewis' chin.

Who could this programme possibly be for?

If you were looking for titillation, well, as erotica goes, the average 9 o'clock movie would serve better. If you were looking to be outraged, you'd have to wait for a couple of episodes before the conversations about types of intercourse kicked in. If you wanted to know how the programme would respond to the cultural phobia about the portrayal of female genitalia in art or whether they would solve the problem of the absence of neutral, friendly words to describe women's bits, or if you wanted to see the notorious episode that dealt with anal sex then you'd have to wait. A million of the first show's viewers decided not to bother. I probably wouldn't have either if it weren't for the fact that I'd been asked to review the show for a monthly magazine and its Stalinesque editor required a mite more patience. Which was rewarded – in small measure to be sure but at least in some measure. *Sex and the City* started to get better... still not what you'd call 'good' but better. And increasingly depressing as the characters' inability to get what they were yearning for became agonizingly clear.

The series followed the every day, every night adventures of four thirty-something Manhattan women – professionals, successful, upwardly mobile and looking for meaningful relationships. And not finding them. At least not yet. So they fill the emptiness in their own way: Sexy Samantha, who's in PR, sleeps with pretty much anyone; Miranda, the lawyer, dallies with a man with whom the sex is great but whom she will definitely not marry; Charlotte, the art gallery buyer, is Ivy League, somewhat preppie and, relatively speaking, inhibited – which allows the show to explore different tastes in sex with a smidgen of emotional empathy. Finally, there's the star of the show, Carrie, who is a sex columnist for a New York newspaper, and uses her own and her friends' experience for her copy. The grim reality is that these women actually want love and marriage but are incapable of negotiating their way to getting it. They make rules like 'never sleep with someone on the first date' and break them; they don't want to be used as sex objects but use men that way; they want exclusivity but their culture assumes that even dating one person at a time is something that has to be negotiated – having sex with someone doesn't necessarily mean that they can legitimately get upset if the man is sleeping with someone else. The act of sex is no indicator of any kind of commitment at all. This is not new but it is still ghastly. And it's not what any of the women really want – convenient perhaps, exhilarating on occasion, but not what they really want. The bottom line is that promiscuity does not deliver. In Manhattan's professional elite, having sex seems the only way to have a chance of getting a committed relationship going but it's only a slim chance.

Interestingly, men are not simply portrayed as lust-obsessed monsters – it is Skipper, Miranda's boyfriend, who leaves her because she won't commit to an exclusive relationship. Still, the show's focus is on what the women think and feel and on how they talk to one another about their adventures. And there is a wonderful sense of female camaraderie about it – four girls, firm friends, talking openly and acceptingly. Refreshingly, there isn't any 'sexual correctness' about the programme – except, of course, that abstinence isn't an option. Charlotte can admit she doesn't like performing oral sex without fear of being mocked. But she suffers for it. Her boyfriend, who had moved from first encounter to exclusive dating with unfashionable haste, dumps her because she won't.

He readily admits that he's found a woman he can share his hopes and dreams with but, hey, no oral sex, no marriage. Realistic? Probably. Loving? No way. Similarly, there is the man who fell in love with an inappropriate woman – he loves her, she loves him but she's not good-looking enough, not really 'anything' enough to fit his friends' or his own expectations of a suitable partner for a successful Manhattanite. Never mind the contents, the packaging is just too drab.

Candace Bushnell's book, on which the series is loosely based, gives little ground for hope. Most of her characters do not get the relationships they want. One of them finds the whole palaver of trying to make monogamous relationships work so utterly futile that he gives up. The TV series maintained its jaunty, upbeat feel and that, combined with its glitzy Manhattan setting, its gorgeous clothes, its even more gorgeous shoes, its beautiful people and its fast-paced editing style made it pretty to watch but, in the end, the TV characters didn't get what they wanted either – Carrie gives Mr Big an ultimatum: commit or that's it. That's it. And Sexy Samantha finally falls in love to the extent that she and Mr Right wait till the absolutely right moment to consummate their love. But, woe, woe, thrice-times woe – the sex wasn't that great.

Mr Right is not big enough to deliver fire-cracker sex, at least not with Samantha – so much for all those books that reassured us men that size doesn't matter. Suddenly Samantha has a choice – a great relationship and not very good sex or no real relationships and lots of good sex. What will she choose? We will never know – unless there's another series.

The tragedy with both the book and the TV series is that neither seems able to face up to the implications of the failure of the relational status quo. Neither condemns this mass relational suicide and neither offers an alternative. Carrie even bewails the fact that she is not the first to nibble her divorced boyfriend's ear – whoa, for a moment she was edging dangerously close to advocating no sex before marriage. Implicitly, there is a yearning for a conservative morality – but will any of these highly intelligent, clear thinking, and acrobatically articulate people have the nous to figure that out? And if even they did, would they dare express it? Might as well expect a man to marry a woman who doesn't like oral sex. How dumb can the clever be? *Sex and the City* had the answer but you didn't need to watch it to find out.

3
Of Micro-Waves and Dish-Washers

It's 3.42 am.

Pitch black outside. Chilly inside.

In the dim distance down the corridor, beyond two half-closed doors the snuffling begins to rise to a whimper . . .

It's going to happen and it's my turn.

The whimper will grow to a cry, to a wail, to an insistent howling crescendo that will make an air raid siren seem as unintrusive as a hamster bell . . . It's going to happen. And it's my turn. Blearily I swivel myself out of bed, gathering momentum like a fighter pilot scrambled . . . and scoot downstairs, flicking the kitchen light on as I slide towards the fridge . . . 15 seconds and counting. The bottle is already in there. I grab it, take two paces to the right, punch the 'open' button and the glass door swings out . . . 19 seconds. I catch it in my left hand and place the bottle on the glass plate with my right ... 21.15 seconds. Push the door gently to ... 23 seconds. And press the one-minute pad. Forty seconds later, I press 'stop' and 'open' and grab the warmed bottle, swivel and dash for the door, flicking the light off as I exit and turn up the stairs ... I can hear the whimpering. Eight seconds later I'm in the room. Two seconds later the bottle is in the mouth ...

Time: 74.5 seconds. Not bad. And good enough. The whimpering subsides, turns to a snuffle, turns to a steady suck. Crisis averted. No one else has been seriously disturbed, no one else knows how my speedy reactions have once more meant that innocent civilians all over our three-bedroomed semi could sleep safe and snug in their beds, oblivious to the crisis averted. In the morning, of course, I will tell them of deeds done in the dead of the night. But it wasn't just me, it was the technology. *Vorsprung durch Technik*. It was the microwave.

In the olden days, before we were given the microwave, in the olden days when the bottle had to be warmed in a pan, in the olden days when it was almost impossible to get it to the right temperature, when I seemed to spend ages cooling it under a running tap, and shook half of it onto my hand testing the temperature, in the olden days when it was impossible to get bottle to mouth in under 3 minutes 17 seconds, long after the howl had already filled every cranny of the house, penetrated beneath duvet and pillow and wakened everyone from their bucolic dreams, leaving us all decidedly crankier the next morning . . . In short, in the olden days, when it was my turn, I failed. The microwave has bestowed better sleep on us all, made our relationships better.

But ten years from now it may not be like that. The 12 year old calls up at 6.30. 'I won't be home till 8.30.' 'But I've made lasagna verde alla siciliana.' 'I'll microwave it when I get home.' The 14 year old doesn't call but turns up at 10.30 and pops it in the machine. The 16 year old turns up at 7 in the morning and has it for breakfast. 'Great lasagna, mum.' Yup, great lasagna but no family meal. Technologies affect relationships – sometimes for good, sometimes for ill. Sometimes saving labour and freeing up time for relationships, sometimes reducing the incentive to eat together. Dishwashers are a great and wonderful thing but just occasionally I miss the opportunity to play with water and call it 'helping out'; I miss the opportunity to just kind of 'be' with someone and burble on about not much at all and then accidentally, effortlessly, it seemed, find ourselves talking about the meaning of life at the beginning of the twenty-first century... as you do.

Relationships are at the heart of life – developing them, nurturing them, enjoying them, protecting them, saving them... The Golden Oldie Rule – love God, love your neighbour – is a rule about relationships. So, one of the key questions we should be asking ourselves is: how does what we do, buy, watch, say, affect our relationships? Will it be likely to bring us closer together or move us further apart? The TV in the bedroom, the TV for the kids, the hired party entertainer that no one will ever see again, the house with the galley kitchen with no room for anyone to sit in, isolating the preparer from the rest of the family or from the mealtime conversation in the next room, isolating the child doing homework from the person preparing their meal. And if a piece of technology has the potential to separate us, how will we anticipate the problem before it arises? Or, more positively, how can we build closer relationships?

One way is to maximize direct contact – being there is better than sending e-mails. It may take two to tango but it doesn't necessarily take two to go shopping or to take the kids swimming. But it's time together and in an over-busy world, time together develops closeness. Those magic moments that bind people together, the great laughs, the shared disasters, the sudden sense of being understood can as easily occur in a traffic jam as in a chi-chi restaurant sipping a Grand Cru St Émilion with the candlelight glinting in your eyes.

Another way to make the most of our relationships is to recognize the value of long-standing relationships – our old acquaintance ain't necessarily our best acquaintance but there's something about old friends – they know just how many times you've floated into the room to announce that you've met the perfect partner, they know how many diets you've been on, they know how you were never, ever a size 12, they know you never actually played the Brixton Academy...just stood at the back and sang along. Old friends are well placed to help you through the tough times and celebrate when the good times are rollin'. However, in a high mobility society, one of the major casualties is our relationships with old friends and indeed with our relatives – we don't live nearby any more. Sure, you may always be best mates with your best mate but you lose something significant when you move to LA for the job and he stays in Swindon. Maybe you have to go, maybe you don't. Money and career shouldn't be the only criteria for the decision: you'll lose continuity and directness of contact with friends, with family . . . Maybe the continuity of those relationships is more important. And even if the move is right, it's as well to recognize that you'll be losing something precious.

Relationships also tend to grow closer if we relate to people in more than one context. At work and in the pub, in the case of a colleague. At home and out in a restaurant, if you're married. And so on. Sometimes it's important to actually see where your partner works – even if it's only a rabbit hutch behind a pillar in a windowless corridor. Sometimes it's important to put faces to the people your husband works with and for them to put a face to you. You're real and that secretary he raves about is 62 not 21. Or she's 24. And on a scale of 1 to 10, she's an 11. Now that you know what he faces every day, it's easier to support him. Or to clobber him round the ear hole with a baseball bat when he says he'll be taking his secretary out for a thank you lunch to a little chi-chi restaurant with a very good St Émilion. That's what friends and spouses are for.

In reality, most decisions we make will have an

effect on our relationships, so nurturing and protecting those relationships is vital. At 3.42 in the
morning and at 3.42 in the afternoon.

4
The Goods, the Ads and the Ugly

I used to work in advertising. So you can trust every word I write.

I may be a Machiavellian manipulator, a sly exploiter of your every weakness, a cunning cultivator of your every lust but at least you can rely on me to be honest, decent, legal and truthful. Or so the advertising tells you.

It's a soft target – advertising. And the temptation is to lay the blame for all the excesses of capitalism and all the hollow superficiality of rampant consumerism at its gleaming doors. For some, advertising is simply the sparkling, Persil-white slopes of the iceberg of materialism that has already fatally punctured the arrogant sides of the Titanic of Western Democracy. If the love of money is the root of all kinds of evil, then advertising is its fertilizer. Indeed. And there's no denying that the West has become more narcissistic, more materialistic, more concerned with self and wealth than with justice and truth. But that said, it's wrong to blame all this on the messengers and to carp on at their techniques, without for a moment examining whether those techniques are actually any different in principle than those of any other major communication medium.

Advertising is criticized for associating its products with good times, good looks and the good life. Well, what do we expect? Advertising is in the advocacy business and the job is to present the product or service in the best possible light. What do we expect? Drink Coke and be alone. Buy Levis but remember they won't change your body shape.

Advertising is accused of creating needs we wouldn't otherwise have. Like what precisely? Think of all the products you buy every week and ask yourself – what's unnecessary? Well, maybe 1.5 ozs of thinly sliced, deep fried, flavoured potatoes for 25p is a questionable purchase in the context of the global distribution of food. But that may be more an issue for individuals than the marketing department of Walker's Crisps. And certainly we should ask ourselves whether the functional attributes of a

BMW Estate can possibly be worth £13,000 or so more than a Vauxhall Omega Estate. But will we buy the BMW because the advertising has projected a clever aspirational image for BMW or simply because everybody knows a BMW is more expensive? And thus a superior status symbol. Well, if you compare the ads, you'll see that the BMW ads are full of information about how well the car is made while some of the Omega advertising takes aspirational pretentiousness to new heights of inanity, quite breathtaking in its vacuousness. For example: 'the advanced multi-link suspension that lets you glide around the testing corners of the Kalambaka mountains. Or the air-conditioning that takes the heat out of those scorching days in St Tropez.'

Advertising is also accused of being more dangerous than the sum of its parts. That is, ignore the fact that some ads are socially responsible, skip past the fact that some ads project a positive view of human relations and put material things in their proper place, forget all that, and remember that the cumulative impact of this crescendo of praise for material goods is a materialistic society. Well, we certainly have one. But if individual ads can get it right, it follows that like most human institutions, it is people that make or break the party... Furthermore, the critics of advertising have never quite solved the problem of how precisely companies are to create mass markets and so make cheaper, often better goods available to more people without mass communications.

Still, advertising does promote values, not just products. It can change social as well as purchase behaviour. It's a big responsibility – many of the ad greats knew that. David Ogilvy knew it. Bill Bernbach knew it. David Abbot knows it. Advertising is not just selling functional benefits – washes whiter, goes faster, tastes better... but also emotional benefits – a caring mum, a virile man, a cool dude. Almost inevitably. Things, after all, have a habit of acquiring emotional associations. I grew up in a Jewish culture. And in Jewish culture chicken soup is not just chicken soup. Chicken soup is the cure for all ills, a panacea. Chicken soup is liquidized mother love. If you're sick and your mother doesn't make you chicken soup, does she still love you? It's a serious question.

Creating associations for products that connect to their product benefits isn't necessarily evil, it's simply an exercise of the imagination. The reality is that if you do six loads of washing a week, sort out the whites from the coloureds, soak the badly stained garments, load the washing machine, unload it, hang the stuff on the line, take it off the line, iron it and fold it and put it in drawers, well, then, you probably wouldn't be emotionally indifferent to the results.

The problem comes when advertising promises benefits it can't possibly deliver – search for the hero inside yourself if you want to find the key to your life – courtesy of a Peugeot 406. Not just the keys to a car but the key to your life. Or in their more recent campaign: don't be afraid to show who you are, your true colours will shine through. Open, honest, vulnerable, authentic – that's what the new 406 tells the world about you. The problem comes when advertising starts to say that you really are a better person if you have this, use that . . . the brand defines the person. As the Rolling Stones put it:

> When I'm watchin' my TV
> And that man comes on to tell me
> How white my shirts can be
> Well he can't be a man 'cause he
>   doesn't smoke
> The same cigarettes as me.

People get judged, welcomed into the club or rejected, depending on the logos they display. This tendency to value a person by their brands is remarkably common and starts remarkably young. A while back Sainsbury's launched their own brand Cola. A TV programme then conducted blind taste tests using Sainsbury's Cola, Pepsi and Coca-Cola. In this particular blind taste test all three brands performed equally well. Then the presenters asked some young people who had actually preferred the taste of Sainsbury's Cola whether they'd buy Sainsbury's Cola. 'No,' came the reply, 'It's naff.' In other words, never mind the taste benefits of Sainsbury's Cola, it doesn't fit with my image . . . and that's what matters to me and to my friends. I'm not buying Cola, I'm buying a statement about my identity, about who I am. Buying the right things becomes a way to establish a worthwhile identity, to tell yourself you're OK. Buying and displaying the right logos becomes a way to belong, to gain the approval of others. Now when 'brands' confer worth on people, when 'brands' give people a sense of psychological wholeness and well-being, then we have turned brands into 'gods'. We worship the brand and, in return, the brand makes us feel worthy. When people feel of greater value because they're holding a Coca-Cola rather than a Sainsbury's Cola, we're in big trouble.

We're in big trouble.

And advertising is partly to blame. Whatever the ads say.

5
Licensed to Thrill

My friend Antony knows more about James Bond than Miss Moneypenny and has marginally more material on Bond than the vaults of MI5. Antony is as wide as Jaws was tall and about as strong, but with better teeth, and he can benchpress an Aston Martin 50 times or so, with or without an oriental gunman in the passenger seat. Antony is 34, married, drives an Astra and is undoubtedly one of the finest teachers of avant-garde, neo-conservative, postmodern hermeneutics in the free world.

And as for me, well, I am Bond, James Bond. Tall, dark and, well, two out of three ain't bad, with a degree in Oriental Languages from Cambridge, the stealth of a leopard, the charm of Cary Grant and a karate chop faster than Bruce Lee on speed. I became James Bond at the age of 8, long before I discovered that spies and centre forwards and rich men in sports cars get the girl at the drop of a monosyllable and a steady smouldering gaze. Maybe it was that music, playing over and over and over again on my mono Elizabethan hi-fi as I wrestled my 8-year-old Blofelds to the playroom floor – dang de de dang dang, dang dang dang, dang de de dang dang, dang dang dang . . . Maybe it was because the first time I remember going to the cinema in the evening was to see *Dr No* down at the local single plex with my Dad. It was a rite of passage in itself – two men out together, the bright lights of the Northwood Hills roundabout, the bustle of other grown-ups. I couldn't have been more than 9.

And I have been James Bond ever since. Now I am 44 and three quarters, married, with three children. I drive an L reg people carrier and work for probably the best think tank in Britain, or at least the best one within a hundred yards of the world's largest record store. But I am still Bond. Never mind that I have read enough Germaine Greer and Bette Friedan and Naomi Wolf to know better, the Bond myth grips me.

Whoever Bond was in the books, the Bond that Cubby Broccoli crafted and Connery defined was what Britain wanted – a British hero. As the Empire dwindled, as the Cold War dropped below zero, it was not the USA with her vast nuclear arsenal and her space programme that would save the world but the lone British hero. One of our chaps. The

CIA's Felix Leiter might make the occasional appearance but he was never much more than a sidekick. Bond would do it. Bond would have to.

Bond is an icon of British charm, good humour, irrepressible optimism, physical strength, martial craft and highly creative personal resourcefulness, and, of course, he is also a gentleman. A gentleman whom blondes preferred. A gentleman who had acquired a vast knowledge of absolutely everything without apparent effort – as knowledgeable of Grand Crus as of the right temperature to serve a Martini. Bond combined this ease with tradition with an ease for the new, without descending into gimmicky trendiness. Q gave him the gadgets but he treated them like toys. In the end, it was not the gadgets that saved him but brains and initiative . . . Superman needed to fly, Hercules needed to be superstrong, Bond is a hero on a human scale, our size even. Why shouldn't one man be clever enough to take on Spectre, skilled enough to fly a Harrier and advanced enough at judo to immobilize a platoon of extras? Bond at his best was believable. In the Connery years particularly. With Roger Moore things changed.

Maybe it was only partly Moore. Maybe it was also that the world had changed. The Cold War turned sideshow by its longevity, the confidence of the West disintegrating in the slow demise and increasing ambivalence of its moral will. The task was there to be done but was it a serious task any more? Bond drifted into irony and veered towards live action cartoon. But he survived. Maybe we still needed a hero to follow. Batman, Superman, Captain Scarlet . . . as heroes, they mostly passed away with childhood. And anyway they were cartoon characters, not 'real' men. Bond was a way of having a 'real' human hero who didn't wear tights or have strings attached. John Wayne's world had long ridden into the sunset. Rambo only lived thrice. Schwarzenegger flexed in different incarnations, certainly a megastar, but just too darned one-dimensional to identify with. Eastwood changed characters and his roles grew increasingly nihilistic as the West reaped the sour fruits of its moral collapse. Bond, however, escaped the limitations of one actor's youth.

What's the great pull? Yes, there is that rich, heady cocktail of lavish sets, big scores, stunning locations, stunning girls, easy unentangling sex, throaty cars, extraordinary opening stunts, the spicy mix of mortal threats – not only dastardly cerebral ingenuity, but also visceral, crunching hand-to-hand combat and the odd deadly beastie thrown in for good measure – snakes slithering in the bathroom, peckish alligators, a shark or two. There is all that. But there is too a marvellous restraint in the violence and the sex that matched Bond's understated style – a strength that didn't have to show off. While Peckinpah *et al.* were sending blood spurting and guts splattering, James didn't need a Magnum 45 to make our day – the neat little Walther PPK would do. And it slipped under a dinner jacket rather more neatly.

Similarly, he may have had sex with 2.5 women per movie, but while starlets were thrashing their way all over other celluloid sex scenes, Bond fans rarely caught more than an appreciative sigh and the occasional view of a well-formed back. Bond, Connery Bond at least, was uncomplicated. However far he pushed his curmudgeonly superiors, there was no doubting his loyalty. He might sleep with the enemy but, unlike Samson, they would never learn his secrets. Sex, too, was uncomplicated, an encounter of willing appreciation, a mutual expression of desire. It was, after all, the 1960s, when it was meant to be simple. It didn't matter to the men that he didn't fall in love, and it didn't matter to the women either. Bond had his own code of honour. He might sleep with someone else's mistress but never his wife, at least not until an old flame turns up in *Tomorrow Never Dies*. And, except for the Tarot-reading Solitaire in *Live and Let Die* he never deceived a woman to get her into bed. And he never gave love to get sex, any more than they ever gave sex to get love. They didn't particularly expect him to stay. Or want him to. They were just grateful for the endorphins. This was free love when the world thought love was free. Except, of course, for Moneypenny.

Moneypenny could be flirted with but not slept with, not because she was the boss' secretary, but because Bond was never going to give her what she really wanted – the house and the children. Moneypenny was the reminder of a time to come perhaps – families and responsibilities and settling down. And so Bond fended her off with the same ease that he attracted women less demanding of heart and soul. Confidence was his keynote. Any time, any place, anywhere Bond could handle himself with deftness and charm.

Yes, there was all that, but above all he had a glorious job – to save the world. The villains may have been caricature grotesques with their scarred faces and PVC hands and third nipples but their ambitions were global and nefarious. It was a black and white world – a world for a hero. A world where one man could make a difference. A world where there was something worth doing. Don't we all long for that?

Here I think is the nub of it all – Bond is a man-sized boy's own hero, a loyal patriot doing his job for his country, a gallant dragoon, still intent on saving the world, still convinced of the worth of what he is saving, incorruptible, daring. An action hero has always been something to be. Maybe we haven't lost our appreciation for people with incorruptible courage and irrepressible resource-fulness.

Thank God for that.

6
Who Wants to Be a Millionaire?

I do. And so does most of the rest of the adult population of Britain, if the weekly sales of Lottery tickets and the viewing figures for Chris Tarrant's programme are anything like accurate.

I bought a Lottery ticket once.

On the principle that if God wanted to make me a millionaire, I wanted to make it easy for him. He blew his opportunity. Now he's going to have to get creative. I bought the ticket on what used to be known as Wednesday, which has now been optimistically renamed Winsday.

I forgot for an instant how our Tory government wilfully and gleefully created a tidy little loadsa-money revenue generator which research world-wide has shown to lead far, far, far more people deeper into poverty than it crowns with infinite riches.

But how a socialist government can countenance

this cynical exploitation of the poor, this corrosive and impoverishing snare ought, of course, to be beyond comprehension. The *Telegraph* called it 'an ineradicable feature of British Life' but in Indonesia the Imams rose against an entrenched government-approved National Lottery and eradicated it. Possibilities abound.

I forgot for an instant that a big win is as likely to ruin your life as to fulfil a lifelong dream.

I forgot for an instant that the Lottery has taken one of the great British myths – the high moral, non-materialistic, Holy Grail-seeking ethos of Camelot – and pillaged it to provide the name for the company that runs it – and even the machines that randomly select the balls. There is no deeper irony than the fact that the Heritage Secretary presides over a process which is systematically destroying the noble heritage of Arthur and Guinevere and Lancelot.

I forgot for an instant the astonishing inanity of the Lottery show which takes an interest in statistics to an all-time low, turning inanimate, numbered balls into personalities, who 'make appearances' in the six number line-up.

I forgot for an instant the ugly little charade that the publicity machine of the Camelooters foist on us – that we are actually doing something to help the poor in our society. This is the Sheriff of Nottingham in Robin Hood's clothing. The Lottery takes a disproportionate amount of money from the poor and gives most of it that doesn't go to government or the Camelooters back into things that the disadvantaged never see, play or do. Only about 5 per cent goes to alleviate poverty.

I forgot for an instant that the Lottery promotes greed, and masks it as giving. Camelot is Grabalot.

Actually I forgot all that for longer than an instant, I forgot all the way from Wednesday to Saturday. Indeed, between Wednesday and Saturday something interesting happened.

I'm walking down the street and I'm working out how I'm going to spend £6 million. A new car. Nothing ostentatious – a Vauxhall Omega Estate perhaps. Then a five-bedroomed house so we can have lots of visitors ... Then invest enough to see our three children through university, if and when the time comes ... And for my wife, a pedigree chum that looks like Lassie. You know, the kind of dog whose ears prick up at the first crunch of my GTi Golf Cabriolet on our long gravel drive as I return from another tough day as Professor of Big Ideas in Europe's premier think tank. The kind of dog who is guaranteed to scamper to the hand-carved, mahogany front door and waggle frantically, springing into my arms as I come through the door, and scrunching my Harvey Nichols linen jacket. And, of course, an au pair girl who speaks eight languages, cooks better than the brothers Roux, has a postgraduate degree in child psychology, advanced coaching certificates in swimming, tennis and skate boarding, and the ability to iron a linen jacket smoother than a snooker table.

I can dream, can't I?

That's what the Lottery sells. People don't really expect to win. What many people buy is not really the chance to win but permission to dream, permission to indulge in a fantasy, when reality is just too tough. The nasty thing about the massive, high-prize, high-hype Lottery we have is that it is a sedative against the reality of much of British life today. And like most sedatives, it not only stops people thinking clearly, it stops people acting decisively to change their circumstances. It's often painful to live in the real world and most of us want something to distract us from that pain, to take it away. Marx understood that when he said that religion was the opiate of the masses. And he recognized that religion could perform a useful function for oppressive regimes – the State using the Church to preserve power. The only way to prevent revolution in hard times is to sedate the masses with the hope of an eternal and much better reward. So it is perhaps no accident that the Lottery was introduced in the midst of a deep economic recession and an even deeper psychological recession. A crisis of hope. In an impatient, secular, if spiritually hungry society, heaven isn't a plausible opiate for the majority of the population. Or if it is, the kingdom of heaven, most of us hope, is years away, while the kingdom of Camelot is only six numbers away. The Lottery is a tool of social control – just like the circuses that the Roman emperors used to quell social unrest. The Lottery gives shape to our week, something to look forward to. And it offers a spurious hope of a transformed life, of a life without the material anxiety of a crumbling society, a life without having to work for £3.60 an hour, a life without having to earn £10,000 a year or so as a qualified nurse and be offered a 1 per cent pay rise one year and a six-month delay the next . . . a life that isn't lived in a neighbourhood where you're afraid to go out at night, or a neighbourhood where every house has burglar alarms.

Back in 1988, an attitude research survey was conducted in London. It revealed that a major underlying concern for British people was concern about the purpose of life – what's it all for? It was from that insight that advertising agency Foote Cone Belding developed the famous Billy Graham campaign 'LIFE. Who can make sense of it?' People just didn't know what the purpose of their life was. And that's a hollow and sometimes frightening place to be. The more you need a transformed life, the more likely it is you will spend your money on the remote possibility of winning the Lottery. You may not expect to win, but you've bought yourself permission to dream. You've bought a paper-thin sliver of hope. And while you're dreaming about the villa, you're not out there demonstrating for a fair day's pay for a fair day's work. 'Forget it all for an instant' is precisely what the Lottery is about. Forget what? Forget reality, forget all the pain, all the pressure, all the anxiety... but just for an instant? I'll say this for the Camelooters – their advertising doesn't over-promise. You can scratch away, but once you have, the odds are overwhelmingly stacked in favour of the itch still being there. An instant later.

The reality of the British Lottery is this: what you see is what you get. And what you see is balls.

We're made for more than this.

7
The Dangerous Sex

It's getting dangerous to be a man. Of course, it always has been.

In the battle of the sexes that raged in the 1960s and the 1970s, not to mention for several millennia before, we men had the upper hand for physical power, political power, economic power, social status, sexual rights, just about everything in fact. But we were always vulnerable to our own insecurities – limited by our machismo, and limited by our limiting of women. Power tends to diminish its owner as well as its victim.

Now one or two things may have changed. There are some women at the top of the business world, some women in the top law firms, some women serving, not just waiting, at the altar, and some women in just about every sphere of public life. But still they tend to be less well paid, less likely to be promoted, and more likely, even if they are working, to do most of the housework and most of the childcare. As Jilly Cooper put it, 'Young wives are in exactly the same position now [as in 1969] having to cook, wash, iron and then make love all night.' And even if a woman does have an enlightened new man for a partner, then she is likely to show more gratitude than a true equality ought to generate. Jilly Cooper again: 'I'm so lucky that Leo cooks supper most nights but I still thank him 59 times.'

It is obviously good news that the simpering, submissive images of woman that filled our TV screens in the 1950s and 1960s have been replaced. But it is bad news that right now, among the plethora of images of women that grace our screens, an increasingly aggressive model of twenty-something female power, dismissive independence and sexual manipulation seems to be emerging. The Madonna of *Material Girl* back in the 1980s knew what she wanted – 'money, that's what I want' – and she knew how to get it. Sexuality was the tool. Today, the daughters of the high priestess of manipulative sex and individualistic materialism are to be seen selling everything from hot chocolate to cars.

The keynote is dominance. And the tool is male desire. Eva Herzegova may have a famous bust and a glorious, open Marilyn Monroe smile but she differs from her forebear in that Marilyn's allure, as Norman Mailer pointed out, was that it looked as if sex with her would be easy, natural. With Eva, you ain't getting it. She knows the effect she's having and she rejoices in the power it gives her. But she isn't available. 'In your dreams,' says one of the ads. And obviously nowhere else. It's great to be in control.

The same trend can be seen in the Nissan Micra ads but without the good humour. A guy borrows his girlfriend's car – because it's such a good car, good enough for a man to be excited about it. And men after all, and even after Germaine Greer, are the arbiters of the best in automotive engineering. Men borrow the car and women exact their terrible revenge. Sticking pins in voodoo effigies of their boyfriend and making him jolt with pain from miles away, throwing him from a first floor window into the swimming pool, and, most notably, welcoming him home in slinky black satin to a candle-lit Bacchanalian feast, consuming it with searing sexual intent, and then with a promise of higher, more esoteric delight, handcuffing this poor unsuspecting man to the bannister. And leaving him there.

Ask before you borrow it.

The man is hoisted with the petard of his own

lust. This is gender judo. And like judo you use your opponent's energy against them. Male desire, so long a weapon used against women, is now the weapon that women turn on men. Not to seduce them for their own pleasure, nor to extricate some morsel of military intelligence for queen and country, but to humiliate. Boys will be boys but girls, well, girls these days are less sugar and more spice.

And if the Micra ads are the extreme, check out Boots No 17 – make-up which is described as 'ammunition'. Check out Guinness' award-winning, grainy black and white, joyous celebration of female physical strength and camaraderie – splendid until you get to the last brilliant but sulphuric line: 'A woman needs a man like a fish needs a bicycle'. Indeed.

Check out Nicorettes. Elegant woman arrives in the bar, sits down, opens her handbag as if to take out a cigarette and immediately a phalanx of flaming lighters are proffered by hopeful male paws. She ignores them all. No courteous thank you. No nod of acknowledgement. She pulls away from the wolfpack faster than a Ferrari from a milk float. She doesn't need a lighter, she doesn't need a man and she doesn't need manners.

This isn't about strength or a woman's ability to be an action hero. It's not about *Tank Girl* or

Sigourney Weaver in the *Alien* films, this is about putting men in their place.

Check out Cadbury's High Lights. Elegant lady in beige in a French bistro-style café with 'The Game of Love' playing in the background:

> The purpose of a man is to love a woman.
> The purpose of a woman is to love a man.
> So come on baby let's start today.
> So come on baby let's play . . .
> the game of love.

Her hot water arrives and she complains to the waiter of a wobbly table. Attractive man behind, elegantly bedecked in the brand's beige and purple colours, sends her a note. Elegant lady reads it, and without so much as a glance behind her to see that the man is elegantly bedecked in the brand's colours, folds his note and places it neatly under the wobbling table leg. Crushed. She may be flattered by the man's attention but she certainly isn't going to acknowledge it.

Twenty years ago such a gallant male gesture might have at least demanded a polite 'no' but these days men, even men elegantly bedecked in the brand's colours, pursue women at their peril. Today's crop of women won't be objects of male desire. They have their own lives and they don't believe that 'the purpose of a woman is to love a man'. Fair enough. But why is the put-down so celebrated? It serves us men right, no doubt. But it is hardly progress. Nor indeed is the way that women have begun to turn men's sculpted torsos, washboard abdomens and contoured pectorals into fetishes in much the same manner that their insightful feminist sisters deplored when we men were doing it to women's bodies.

Women have, in the words of the original Charlie ads, come a long way, but if many of the contemporary images are a guide, they may end up in the same nasty, sexist cul-de-sac that men are in. Which only goes to show, as indeed we have long learnt in the political arena: liberation is much, much better than slavery but it is no guarantor of authentic freedom. The liberation of women is a great opportunity for humankind. Alas, if all that happens is that the image-makers raise a generation of women who think that the zenith of femininity is to teach men a lesson.

8
A Little Alarm
about Calm

Adults are meant to be stronger than this.

This one isn't.

And neither are some 715,641 others. In Britain alone.

About 15 years ago supermarket checkouts used to be the place where you'd find multi-hued mountains of Mars Bars and Milky Ways and Smarties and Rolos and Fruit Pastilles and every possible sweetie thing dear to the hearts of kiddies. Innocent and pure they would enter the supermarket, calm and open-faced and unsuspecting they would toddle down the aisles, their little hands peacefully and ever so obediently holding on to their mother's fresh-pressed summer frock. Patient they were as she turned over a hundred tomatoes to choose four, approving as she weighed six identically priced

cucumbers to ensure she selected the heaviest
one, glowing as she chatted to Dorothy about the
challenges of child-rearing in the early 1980s...
Until...stacked up to the left of them, stacked up
to the right of them – into the valley of temptation
rode the six year olds...Suddenly, their eyes
bugged out three feet in front of their noses,
suddenly the fresh-pressed summer frock was
being pulled half way off their mother's shoulder,
suddenly the gentle parental 'no' was met with a
glare of volcanic hatred and Stalingrad defiance,
suddenly the face had turned ketchup red with
rage...

Day by day, week by week parents were being
led like lambs to the slaughter...the anticipation
of the confrontation at the checkout stealing all joy
from the shopping experience; the ghastly checkout
Catch 22:

Either
you are humiliated in front of a hundred
strangers because you can't stop your toddler
screaming at a decibelage to make a Manic Street
Preachers concert seem as hushed as the Reading
Room of the British Library,

or
you are humiliated in front of a hundred

strangers because you can't stop your toddler screaming at a decibelage to make a Manic Street Preachers concert seem as hushed as the Reading Room of the British Library and then you give in and let them have a whole tube of Smarties.

'Parents these days,' you hear them think, 'they let their children get away with anything. No wonder British industry isn't competitive – we've brought up a generation who think they can get what they want with a little bit of whinging.' Eventually, it was parents, aided by the Chuck Sweets off the Check-Out Campaign, who whinged in droves – and the supermarkets capitulated. Nowadays, if you find anything at all on the checkout, it's likely to be a more adult selection of goodies – cheapish magazines, sugar-free gum, and so on.

So who now wears the crown of King of the Checkout Impulse Purchase? Answer: bookshops. And who do they snare? Adults. Without so much as a whimper or a tugged cuff. With no mother to suppress the infantile urge we pick up a little card, a minuscule little book of poems for lovers, a minuscule little volume of quotations for cooks ... and, more than almost anything else in the last year or so, we picked up Paul Wilson's minuscule *Little Book of Calm*. Some 715,641 copies to date. A psychological sweetie. Suck a page of this and you'll feel better. Smart marketing.

I wanted to hate this book.

First of all, it was so successful for such little effort – 99 per cent marketing and 1 per cent content. But as The Good Book says: thou shalt not covet thy neighbour's marketing department, nor their opportunistic intelligence, nor their canny ability to turn five talents into ten.

I wanted to hate this book because I was sure it would be affably authoritative, deferentially guruesque, warm, New-Agey – a basic stress management guide in pastel packaging. Well, if those are grounds for hatred, *The Little Book of Calm* delivers a continent, but it has to be said there's some wisdom here, some wit here, some insight here. Common-sense tidbits like: 'Milk helps you relax and become calm. (It is rich in calcium, a muscle relaxant, as well as an amino acid called tryptophan, a powerful natural sedative.)' So we get sound advice about diet (herbal tea and fruit) and exercise (run) and sleep (more) and controlling our physical environment – I'm off to buy a plant or two to oxygenate my office. We get little stress control tricks like using worry beads, little time management tricks like 'Say no' and little mind control tricks like 'Picture yourself on an idyllic

South Pacific Island.' We get little lifestyle tricks like 'live simply' and little character development tricks like 'forgive'. Not much wrong with most of it really except that I'm not convinced that doing all of these things would really deliver the goods. You can't decide to stare at the fish tank while your three year old and your six year old are playing tug of war and your hamster is the rope. You can't just think your way into positively viewing bereavement or the threat of redundancy. You can't just wave a bowl of lentils at a serious illness and expect it to go away.

What the book promises is 'a path to inner peace'. And the way you get there is this: 'When you feel troubled simply let this book fall open – let your intuition guide you – and you will see the most effective way for you to find calm at that particular moment. Trust your intuition and you will become calm.' Well, now, that is a pretty big claim, isn't it? Inner peace by just letting the page fall open? I did that, and the page fell open at some advice about getting more Vitamin B from wheatgerm and peas . . . which, as you can imagine, just made me more angry. So I tried again. This happened, honest. The page fell open at 'Watch your Head. Most stress and anxiety is the result of what happens inside your head, rather than what happens to your body.' Fair enough and right at this moment not inaccurate, but it goes on, 'Take comfort in the fact that most things which take place in your thoughts never eventuate.' As if 715,641 copies of the Little Pastel Book wandering around the British Isles boosting sales of wheat-germ and lentils isn't enough to have taken place already. And besides, my intuition was telling me that this *Little Book* was opium in medicinal packaging, pain relief, not cure.

I wanted to hate this book because I was pretty sure it would be totally unrealistic about human nature – you can fix every problem you have all by yourself, with, of course, just a little help from the author. Well, if only Adam and Eve had read *The Little Book of Calm* they would never have had any desire for a different fruit, particularly since they would have had no idea how much Vitamin A or B it would contain. If only Hitler, if only Saddam, if only I . . . Not that there aren't some things which sound like paraphrases from the Bible: 'Most worries are future-based. They revolve around things that, in most cases, will *never* happen. Concentrate on the present and the future will take care of itself.' Compare that to something Jesus said: 'Therefore do not worry about tomorrow, for tomorrow will worry about itself.' But there's a life and death difference between the worldview of *The Little Book of Calm* and the universe of the Good Book. And the difference is contained in that little 'therefore' in front of 'do not worry'. Because, the Good Book says there's a Father God who loves you, therefore don't worry. Don't worry because there's a Father God who created you and if you're in relationship with him, then you'll have eternal peace.

What's wrong with *The Little Book of Calm* is not so much its advice about this and that and the other but its basic assumptions. *The Little Book* thinks humans can crack this life business all on their own, *The Little Book* thinks that we all have the power to forgive and forget and live simply and generously and without greed or worry all on our own. *The Little Book* thinks that humans can find authentic inner peace without God . . . and according to the Good Book of Peace what *The Little Book of Calm* thinks is cause for considerable alarm.

9
The 24-Hour Society and a Little Austrian Inn

Half way between Salzburg and Innsbruck there's a snug and pretty little town called Mittersill. It has its own medieval castle high on the mountain with wonderful views down the valley to the east and wonderful views across the snow-laden slopes that stretch south towards Italy. Kitzbuhel is 20 minutes away, up over the pass. Just off the main square with its plashing fountain there's a successful inn with two dining rooms – one gleaming and smart and cosmopolitan, the other smaller with a traditional Austrian ambience.

We've come for supper.

Three of us: my wife, fluent in Swiss German, a Canadian academic also fluent in German who spends half his year here, and me, clanking along with my rusty 'S' level in high German. There's something on the menu that none of us can decipher

– *Lammschlörgell*. We ask. It's a local word for leg of lamb. Probably someone born more than 15 miles away couldn't have deciphered it either. This particular leg of a lamb, it turns out, is one of four that came from a lamb that used to gambol and frolic on a farm just up and beyond the castle.

'It's important to know what you're eating,' the owner tells us, 'because if you don't like it I can go and tell the farmer.'

The inn closes for three weeks in the summer – at the height of the tourist season. Why would he do that?

'What other time would you want to take your holiday with your family?' he asks.

Up the hill, there's another nice restaurant but the owner doesn't accept credit cards. He's been told that if he took a card or two he'd get a lot more business. 'I have enough business,' was his reply.

It's the way things were: people using words that only locals understand – tangy little words like *Lammschlörgell* that probably rolled spontaneously off some farmer's tongue after a particularly del-*ischi*ous leg; going on holiday in the tourist season because it's the best time to go on holiday; being satisfied with enough.

Quaint.

I'm in the front seat of a Mondeo mini-cab with a driver who only works for business accounts. He could upgrade to a Merc and command higher fares but he says, 'I make what I need.'

Enough. Now there's a novel concept. It is our general inability to say 'enough' which is, according to many, driving us all inexorably towards the 24-hour society – the society where the shops never close, where you can go to the post office at three in the morning, have your teeth done at four, shop at five, go dancing at six . . . a society where people will be working to give us what we want whenever we want it . . . Shoppers' heaven. Which is apparently what we all want.

I doubt it. But the trouble with a global economy is that there's always a customer awake somewhere and some of us will have to be awake to serve them.

Whatever we wanted 30 years ago, whatever we really want now, many of us actually need to shop, go to the dentist, visit the post office outside normal working hours because more of us are working during normal opening hours. We want the shops to stay open. Except when we're the ones behind the counter. We've bought our kids the Winnie the Pooh pyjamas but it's someone else reading them the story – the one about Pooh not being able to get his buttocks out of Rabbit's House and go home – and all because he's eaten so much honey. Ah, that's the trouble with greed – it keeps you out late. But I wonder: whose greed is it anyway? Ours? Or the companies'?

It's true that some of us may have chosen the lure of lucre over time with family, time with friends, time walking the dog but my hunch is that many of us have been forced to sacrifice our time walking the woofer so that we can make enough money to live with a modicum of social dignity in a consumerist culture. There's a body of evidence around to suggest that we need to earn a great deal more in real terms now than we did in the 1960s to deliver the same standard of living. There are also a lot more children living in poverty than there were 20 years ago. Still, even if we are on the whole better off materially than we were 40 years ago, are we any happier? As Tony Blair said in 1995: 'We enjoy a thousand material advantages over any previous generation, and yet we suffer a depth of insecurity and spiritual doubt they never knew.' No social commentator seriously questions this. But few offer an alternative.

Leon Kreitzman, a social commentator and the author of a fine book called *The 24 Hour Society*, admits that consumerism has not delivered psychic health. He admits that the contemporary workplace is not simply insecure, it assaults people's sense of self-identity and produces higher levels of anxiety. He admits that 'most businesses have not found a way to help individuals balance work and family priorities.' He admits that families 'will have to take more care in planning joint events', that the family 'will have to work harder to maintain itself as a cohesive unit'. In other words, he admits that this glorious 24-hour society is going to be even harder on relational depth and personal belonging. This is not a happy thought for anyone who has glanced at the divorce statistics or the number of prescriptions for anti-depressant drugs.

But we are powerless to change it because we have to buy things to give us a sense of identity. And to buy, we'll work anytime, anyplace, anywhere – for as long as it takes. As a society, we have bought consumerism – hook, copy line and logo – and there's no way back.

The key question remains unaddressed: can a society that vaunts consumerist values above all else deliver anything like human fulfilment? The answer is self-evidently 'no'. But that's what we have today.

And since almost everyone with any power – trade unions and governments alike – believe in 'market solutions', there is no opposition. A few may be able to downshift City jobs for carpentry in the lush green of the Caernarvon hills but most of us don't have the luxury of asking: can I change my job and work for less? For most of us, the real question is: could I find another job that I could do and still make any kind of living? We're caught.

Our technologies and our structures are changing faster than our ability, and more importantly, our will to assess their impact on our emotional, mental and spiritual health. In reality, there are precious few people thinking through how we can make our technologies work to create a society which leads to greater overall human flourishing, to a way of life and work which will make us rich in relationships and joy, not just designer mobiles.

This is the challenge before us. This is the research that really needs funding. And if Bill Gates and BT and Co cared as much about the future of humankind as they say they do, they'd be funding that thinking. But they aren't. Because there's no money in it.

Aha, there's an idea: if only we could find a way to develop a product or a service that delivered genuine social and relational fulfilment . . . we'd make a fortune. Did you hear that, Bill?

10
How to Have an Affair

Another day, another city. Another smart hotel, another bar. Another quick drink at the end of the evening. A little dash of gin. A little sparkle in the eye. A little loneliness. A sprinkling of confidences, a few intimacies exchanged as bait, the tentative preparations for something more. And then something more. And so, so much less.

A lot of people meet the people they are going to marry at work. Presumably if they were working somewhere else they might well have met someone else they wanted to marry. And if you're likely to meet someone you want to marry in a fairly large workplace, the chances are that you might meet someone you could have an affair with.

Workplaces are in some ways like villages. And like villages they have their own culture, their own beaux and belles in their own closed corporate world. And how remote from everything outside that world can sometimes seem.

For us, they were the Titania and Oberon of our mid-Manhattan dream. He, tall, well built, blond, square chinned – a paragon of the American male. And our senior day-to-day client. She, our leader: long, leggy, with hair that fell in dark cascades onto her shoulders – and were the skirts just a shade too short for corporate life? We wondered. Certainly, the two of them produced great work, led us all to produce great work. But at social events they sparred and sparkled. There was electricity between them. And to us all it seemed OK. Seemed somehow appropriate, exhilarating even. We wondered, as they danced round each other at a party, whether their king and our queen would one day conjoin. Somehow the fact that he was married and had three children was a hazy detail that had slipped over the edge of our conscious horizon. Here, where our two tribes met, in the sheen of five star hotels, moving to the bass throb of the disco, here, far from the madding domestic suburbs, here these two were Cinderella and her prince, not moths fluttering round the consuming candle of adultery.

I'm at an evening client and agency party. One of the senior agency people is there with his wife. It's going to be awkward to meet her. I know something she doesn't: her husband is having an affair with one of my colleagues. Everyone there from the agency knows this. We're introduced, we talk and all the time I'm thinking the kind of thoughts you think – a mixture of pity, of ghastly voyeuristic fascination, of looking for a reason why it might be her fault, or his. Comparing one woman with another. And all the while having that dirty, clammy feeling that I too am deceiving her, that one day she will find out and one day she will know that we were all silent partners in his betrayal.

Nowadays so many people work a long way from home that it is easy for us to lose that sharp awareness that they have another life out there. And that we do too. So, in the rough and tumble of the working world we find ourselves talking to our bosses or secretaries or colleagues and sharing with them first the joys and struggles, the triumphs and failure – encouraging them, empathizing with them, complimenting them on good work, new clothes, and so on. And sometimes appreciation drifts into flirtation. Pretty soon, with all that

common purpose, all the teamwork, all the adren-
alin that might go into a particular project we find
ourselves with a particular friend. A friend who
becomes our tribal spouse. And then if we're not
careful as the momentum of appreciation, attraction
and circumstance gathers speed, our adulterous
partner.

Innocent enough are most of our relationships
at work. Good friendships perhaps. Not a reason
for paranoia. But certainly a reason for caution. We
are all vulnerable at the wrong moment to the right
person. In Pollack's film *The Firm* Tom Cruise is
happily married to the right woman but the
Machiavellian firm are determined to compromise
him. They dangle a sensual woman at him on a
business trip down in the Cayman Islands. He can
resist that. But as he walks off down the beach, he
sees a man attacking a woman and runs to her rescue.
She has sprained her ankle and he binds it. She is
gorgeous and grateful and confesses to him that
she had been with the other man for the money,
confides that she works in a travel agency so that
she can imagine what it might be like to be rich.
Cruise, like her, was once poor. He shares the
same emotional wound she does, the same need to
escape poverty, to find value in personal net worth.
He empathizes with her pain deeply, because for

him that pain still remains. She exploits this emotional link to seduce him. He, after all, has already been softened up by playing the role of white knight galloping to the rescue of the damsel in distress. Men are often most sexually vulnerable when a woman is emotionally vulnerable. Every cell in our male DNA is programmed to protect. And how quickly tender protection turns to physical affection. So it is that happily married, faithful Cruise falls and fornicates on the beach. Importantly, as the film points out, it wasn't just sex, it was something much more intimate – an exchange of pain and balm. Adultery, like marriage, is rarely simply fuelled by desire.

He was very attracted to her. A Christian man attracted to a Christian woman in a Christian mission organization. She wasn't doing anything to fan that attraction and he wasn't saying anything or doing anything to let her know. But she was his PA and he was finding it increasingly difficult to concentrate, increasingly difficult to believe that he might not one day do something that he didn't want to do. He was married and so was she. What should he do? He had prayed about his desire and it had not abated. So he went to his boss and explained the situation. His boss took it seriously and suggested they try to transfer the lady. So she went to work for a more senior person in the organization and was never told about her former boss' problem. A radical solution perhaps but a solution that took seriously the power of sexual attraction. Maybe we all ought to be able to control our desires all of the time but it's wise to recognize that, however happy we might be, however far from a mid-life crisis, however well our spouses understand, there are probably one or two people it's safer not to go into the stationery cupboard with.

There's a rumour out there that an affair can do wonders for a marriage – a little tonic not a pernicious toxin. The divorce courts are full of people who believed that rumour. And our houses are full of children whose fathers don't live with them any more.

11
No Flowers Please, We're British

Finally, the police took down the white tarpaulins in front of Jill Dando's house. Her front door had been removed for further forensic examination. In its place there was what looked like a plain sheet of unpainted plywood – like some condemned house that the Council had boarded up. Once again millions mourned the death of an English rose – another tallish, open-faced, open-hearted blonde with the knack of making ordinary people who had never met her feel a connection. This was not the accidental death of a heroine in a speeding saloon – a death that could be explained – but an assassination, it seemed – a single bullet to the head from a 9mm pistol. Could this possibly be a professional hit on the girl next door? Is anybody safe?

Once again there were flowers on the streets of London. Our way of marking death, at least celebrity deaths, has changed. For a nation with such restrained private, mourning rituals, at least in the South, our mourning of public figures will no

longer be constrained. We will not abide by the old
protocols – 'no flowers please', 'send cheques to
such and such a charity', 'family only' ... We will
make the pilgrimage, leave a card, write in the book
of remembrance.

In the aftermath of Diana's death, the right-wing
think tank, the Social Affairs Unit, told us that we
British had become a nation of self-indulgent
sentimentalists, that nothing revealed it more clearly
than the outpouring of grief at Diana's funeral and
her quasi-canonization. It told us that our institutions were fake, our church services blasphemous
shams, that we had become a society obsessed with
self-fulfilment at the expense of duty.

And they had a point. And maybe more than
one. It's true that self-fulfilment is the aim of many
of our lives – my pleasure, my psychological ease
take precedence over most duties and obligations:
my promises to my wife, my commitments to my
children. It's true that some of our religion has
become superficial. It's true that style has become
more important than substance. It's true that our
civilization is finding it increasingly difficult to tell
image from reality. It's true that many people feel
themselves to be victims of society and won't accept
responsibility for their own circumstances ... but
it's not the whole truth.

A nation, or a great part of it, cried at Diana's

funeral, cried because for 18 years or so most of us who read the non-'quality' newspapers had seen her picture three or four times a week, learned every detail of her life, knew every dress she wore, followed every event she attended...a nation knew her, and mourned. A nation also mourned for the death of a dream, of a princess for whom the fairy tale turned into a nightmare. We mourned for a wife, perhaps always put second in the heart of a husband, trying to do his duty for his country by marrying a virgin. We mourned for the children often separated from parents – a common failure in our society, a failure all the more to be mourned because it is ours too... We cried for our own disappointments, our broken marriages, our unhappy relationships, our shattered dreams.

We cried too because as a nation it was a time to pour out the pent-up grief for Hillsborough and Bulger and Dunblane, for the brutality of the Thatcher years – the politics of the trickle-down effect, of deep depression, of every human for themselves, of the corrosive anxiety of being reduced to a unit of production. So we mourned for a woman whose smile and concern said that this was not so – like the concern that a priest has for a flock, some of whom he may hardly know but loves nevertheless. No wonder we cried for Diana – at least she cared.

We cried because God created humans with hearts as well as heads. We cried because all was not right with the world. We cried because we know there ought to be a better way, because we wanted the dream to come true, because we still have a memory of Eden, or at least a yearning for a new heaven and a new earth, a place where disappointment will end. We cried because we hoped that Diana and Charles, at least, might have lived a charmed life for us. And we could live it vicariously. But it was all a myth. And when the comforting myth died with the real woman, lots of people turned to God – for a while anyway. The atheists must have been wringing their hands in despair, despite all the secularism of society. Suddenly people were talking God-talk. Suddenly, on that funeral day, people serving in motorway cafés stopped to pray the Lord's Prayer... and hoped that there was someone there.

The outpouring of grief over Diana was genuine but the most important thing that it reveals is not a society that is fake but a society that, despite its sophistication, will only be truly satisfied by the real thing.

Two years on that hasn't changed. Two millennia on that hasn't changed. Why would it?

12
The Most Admired Man in the World

His humility is breathtaking.

But for the last 50 years he has been the dominant figure in Gallup's poll of the World's Ten Most Admired Men – appearing an unmatched 41 times.

I met him once.

It was at an international press conference in New York. When he arrived, there was no big announcement, he just walked in with two or three of his colleagues. As he did, I felt we should all stand up.

No one did.

I didn't either.

I wish I had.

He didn't read out his press statement – we had it anyway – he just answered questions. Some of the questions were factual; some reflected the concerns of particular communities; some, it seemed to me, were about the spiritual struggles of the journalists themselves. No doubt he knew that. He was very gracious. And very agile.

His press officer wound things up. The TV lights dimmed and the sound was turned off but he said 'Thank you for coming' into the dead microphone. Not many heard. But he said it. Then there was a queue to talk to him. I joined it. I told him the story of how he had encouraged my wife years before we met. At the time Katriina wasn't a dignitary, no important wheel in the organization, she was just a twenty-something volunteer he'd been introduced to. Katriina had said that for the two minutes she'd talked to him she'd felt like she was the only person in the world, that his attention had been totally on her. Oh, yes, the room had been full of important national figures at the time but his attention had been totally on her. Like a channel for the love of God.

He asked me where I came from. I told him about the ads I was doing and the place I worked. 'I love that College,' he said, rocking back in his chair and smiling. He did – he became a patron a year later.

Afterwards, I reflected that it had been just as Katriina had said. For two minutes there had been no one else in the world, there, at an international press conference in a New York hotel, surrounded by people. Just me and the most admired man in the world.

Of course, most people don't get that close. Most people have heard of him because they've seen or heard him speak. In fact, he's spoken to more people than any speaker in the history of the world. Some experts don't consider that he's a particularly gifted orator but he's got something to say and you know that he believes it. And people's lives are changed – people from virtually every nation on earth – young, old, religious, non-religious, intellectuals and people who can't read.

Most people don't get that close to him but maybe even when he's a disembodied voice coming out of the radio, maybe even when he's a speck at the other end of an auditorium, people still sense he cares about them. With lots of history's so-called great people, the closer we've got to them, the less admirable they've seemed. Not so with him – the more you find out, the more remarkable he seems. On him, there is the mark of true greatness: true greatness does not diminish others but affirms them. True greatness does not steal our identity and sense of worth, true greatness gives. And, as Billy Graham taught me, true greatness is breathtakingly humble.

13
Keeping Up With the Bridgets

If you are a man and happen to be wondering what happened to old-fashioned women who just wanted to be swept off their feet by a knight in a shining Golf GTi – wonder no longer... postmodern, post-feminist woman is, if Helen Fielding's *Bridget Jones' Diary* is to be believed, alive and well, making a decent living all over London and waiting for your e-mail. Indeed, it's almost as if *The Female Eunuch* and all the feminist literature of the 1970s had never been written. Like Ally McBeal, Bridget Jones' American counterpart, post-feminist woman can make a living without a man, she can make a statement without a man but, unless she's lesbian, there's the rampant suspicion that she won't have a life until the One arrives. Even one of *Company*'s covers was emblazoned with the promise of an article to help you discern if he's 'the One'. Romance blooms on.

Bridget Jones' Diary sold over a million copies and spawned a new category of 'there are two types of people in the world' – viz. those who like Bridget Jones and those who don't. I did. Just. The *Diary* is *Pride and Prejudice* for the 1990s – Jane Austen meets Nick Hornby. Our heroine – obsessing about weight, cigarette consumption, alcohol intake, and the purchase of Instants – is a 30-year-old single woman in pursuit of an eligible man for love, sex and we'll see what happens. Burdened by low self-esteem, irritated by parental pressure to get fixed up, convinced by the ubiquity of commitment phobia among the entire male sex, Bridget Jones veers between despair, elation, cynicism, lust, moony infatuation, careful strategic relationship planning and impetuous abandon. Funnily, believably, and I'm told by some of my female friends, quite realistically.

If the comparison with Austen is far-fetched in terms of deft characterization, there are certainly conscious parallels and counterpoints in terms of the plot line – Bridget is dallied with by a thorough bounder but ends up with her very own Darcy – a rich barrister – who rescues her family from financial ruin. In this modernized version, however, it's not a younger gullible sister who is taken in by a smooth operator but her mother – intent on sexual liberation and a career in TV, after 30 years of marriage and homemaking. Things change but not that much.

Bridget Jones is a fine sketch of a young woman caught in the dilemmas of singleness, with well-intentioned but not always wise friends and a yearning for authentic love. Or at least a boyfriend who isn't sleeping with someone else. Like Hornby's *High Fidelity*, this is not great literature but it's funny and sad and gives a portrait of just how difficult it is to develop relationships in the anonymity of the city, just how difficult it is to find a man you can trust, just how hard it is to be single when all your friends are coupled up. Unlike Hornby's *High Fidelity*, I ended up caring about the leading character and hoping that she and Darcy lived happily ever after, with no need for the addictive purchase of Instants and the calorie binges that stalk emotional upset. But it wasn't at all clear that that was the way it would work out.

Alas, for the uncertainty of our relationships.

But hurrah for the persistence of the monogamous urge. Of the desire to abandon oneself to loving The One. There is hope through relationship. Hope in the kind of relationship that is deeper than even the best friends can offer... hope through a relationship where we can be known and be accepted and where we can offer acceptance to the other. Hope in depth and intimacy, not merely in the convenience of having someone to take to dinner parties and sleep with afterwards.

Bridget Jones is by no means alone in this yearning for The One. On BBC2's *Bridget Jones' Night* Mariella Frostrup, blonde, single, thirty-something and, as far as I'm concerned, unbelievably not seeing anyone at the moment, chatted with five other thirty-something singles about Bridget. In the end, the conversation came round to the question: would any of them give up their jobs and follow The One if he had to go to Outer Mongolia? In other words, would love or career win? The journalist Janine di Giovanni was unapologetically clear – if it's The One, she'd go anywhere. She'd find something to do – a bit of writing, a bit of gardening... The committed relationship becomes more important than anything else – the foundation for a life, not a bolt-on accessory. Suddenly I found myself thinking, well, if she'd do that for me, go there for me, well, then it would make me feel like trying to renegotiate with my boss for a posting to Beijing, or somewhere a bit less remote, somewhere that might offer her a bit more. Being totally loved calls forth the desire to seek the best for the beloved.

You don't need to read *Bridget Jones* to know that contemporary courtship rituals are highly destructive and that sexual freedom has led to a great deal more emotional pain than the *Cosmos* and *GQ*s would have us believe, but it is startling to see just how persistent the desire for monogamous commitment is and just how explicitly contemporary women are prepared to express it. God may not be in the picture at all, and the means to their avowed goal may presume a sexual licence not all would affirm but the yearning for The One, and a One who is not simply a prince but a committed prince who is eager to serve his beloved, is no bad platform to begin to explore the basis for love in marriage.

Meanwhile back in metropolis, there are a lot more 'lonely people' out there than John, Paul, George and Ringo ever foresaw. It's a loneliness at the centre of society, not out on the margins. It's made sharper by the gnawing sense that the chances are that it won't change much. And if it does, it won't change for long. Statistics suggest that around 40 per cent of adult women now live without men. That's what the stats say, but they don't tell you the whole story, do they? Ask the Bridgets.

14
Vergin' on Sainthood?

A year or so ago a poll revealed that Richard Branson was the most admired man in Britain. It also revealed that no one else came close – not Tony Blair, not Prince Philip, not Alan Shearer, not Desmond Lynam, not Tim Henman, not George Carey, not Ted Hughes, not Chris Evans, not Anthony Hopkins, not Cliff . . . Branson eclipsed them all.

And you can see why. Branson has a formidable set of qualities – he's a great businessman but makes business fun. He's made pots of money but apparently at no one else's expense. His most famous ventures have involved taking on the big guys, offering the buyer at the till better value and managing to hang on, hang on, hang on long enough to survive. He took on the big record shops and won, he took on the big record labels and won, he took risks on all kinds of artists and sometimes won, most famously with Mike Oldfield's *Tubular Bells*. He took on the British Rubber Company's virtual monopoly of the condom business and gave people sex for less. He took on British Airways and, unlike a host of famous and celebrated small carriers like Laker, he's still flying. He took on Coca-Cola and Pepsi and now has the third largest selling branded Cola in Britain. He's a business David taking on Goliaths – and how we love the underdog. He made a bid for the Lottery, wanting to give rather more of the loot to charity than his competitors – and lost. Well, maybe he was naïve – lotteries have never been about helping the needy, have they? He's a risk-taker but he's not just a taker.

Interestingly, Branson's initiatives are not focused in one area – what business goes from records to condoms? And since when has the airline business been an appropriate platform for a fast-moving package goods business like soft drinks? What connects Branson's businesses is verve and value and trust – 'fun, fizz and freedom', as he puts it. His positioning is psychographic: you fly Virgin and you know you're flying an airline with a personality – highly professional, rather more picky about making sure those bags are actually under your seat but with bouncy pop jaunting through the speakers and a billion films to choose from. In an old Virgin ad an elegant business woman makes her way through the terminal as Frank Muir's laconic voice-over intones: 'Virgin has a rather different view of corporate man than your traditional airline.' Indeed. At the time, BA's campaign was all about tough men (and one silent, tea-sipping woman) sitting round a vast boardroom table commenting on the impending success of their conspiratorial plans to scupper a rival. Given all that was to transpire between Virgin and BA the word 'irony' seems to leap from the keyboard. And if Virgin Trains aren't yet running on time as often as Branson would like, they're running on time rather more often than they used to – and in the end, Richard will fix it.

On the surface it all seems rather splendid – business doesn't have to be boring, products don't have to be that expensive, personal money management doesn't have to involve 83 different institutions ... And splendid it has been, partly because Branson is a fantastic publicist: he'll dress up as a bride to launch a bridal wear company, wear a bowler to launch a bank – he'll do almost anything to give the photographers an interesting picture. When he launches his fast-food restaurant chain, he'll probably turn up as a dancing tomato. But there's more to his success than good publicity – there's gritty determination and hard work and picking the right people. The word is that Branson's employees like working for Virgin companies – he keeps the companies small and lean and the team spirit is terrific. The word is that Branson's employees get paid slightly less than Branson's competitors – Branson runs a tight ship but it's a ship people want to sail on. After all, there's more to life than money. And Branson's got both – money and a life. Though he seems to take more risks with the latter than the former, as his ballooning adventures reveal.

When the misleadingly titled *Losing My Virginity* came out, so inevitably did the muckrakers. Depending on which newspaper you read, you learned rather more about the underside of Branson's private life than maybe you wanted or needed to know. The hypocrisy of some sections of the media is only exceeded by their greed – peddling muck while condemning it. In his autobiography, Branson is open about his 1970s' promiscuity, direct about his adultery and perhaps rather too enthusiastic about the jaunty deceptions of his earlier years. He's not gay but is relaxed about homosexual practice and runs a gay nightclub called *Heaven*. Not everyone would agree with his position but it seems to stem from compassion and solidarity with the outcast, and perhaps a misplaced optimism about what all these new freedoms will bring. He is, after all, a man of his times – and like those times he wanted to see a different world. The student newspaper he co-founded collapsed but the help line that grew out of it continues today. He lends his name to a charity or two, and in the Gulf War he flew tens of thousands of blankets into Jordan to help the refugees. And then he personally organized the release of 200 hostages from Iraq on one of Virgin's planes – not a bad coup for a businessman with only four 747s. And not a small risk for an airline with only four 747s. If that 747 had been destroyed or held in Baghdad, Virgin would have gone bust. Branson doesn't seem intent on ripping anyone off, he doesn't seem to take himself too seriously, and he's not judgmental.

Branson is no Saint Mother Teresa but he's a balloon-ride to Andromeda IV away from the self-centred, money-grubbing ruthlessness of the stereotypical tycoon. *Losing My Virginity* may be a religion-free zone but Branson's is still a life to ponder. As one early saint put it,

'... if anything is excellent or praiseworthy – think about such things'.